Holding Space: My Story of Grief, Remembering, and Thriving after Traumatic Loss

By Arielle Jordan, LCPC

First Edition: September 2023

Holding Space: My Story of Grief, Remembering, and Thriving after Traumatic Loss/ Arielle Jordan

ISBN: 978-1-943616-56-5

Publisher: MAWMedia Group, LLC
Los Angeles | Reno | Nashville

DEDICATION

I dedicate this book to my late daughter, Jordyn Da'yana Hammonds. You are my WHY. I will forever miss you, baby girl. Although your life ended far too soon, I promise to keep living for you, carrying your light in my heart.

To my late dad, Michael Jordan, I love you and am determined to finish what I start, making my mark on the world in your honor. Your love and support remain with me every step of the way.

To my mother, Bettie Thomas, thank you for allowing me to share a part of your story. You have overcome numerous challenges in life and served as an inspiration for me to persevere and keep pushing forward.

To my brother, Adrion, thank you for always bringing laughter into my life and being a sounding board for my ideas. Your presence and support mean the world to me.

To my brother, Garrett, thank you for watching my dog whenever I needed a mental break. Your help allowed me to find moments of peace during the writing process.

To my best friends, Rita and Jazzi, thank you for standing beside me through thick and thin. Your unwavering encouragement and celebration of my wins have been a vital source of strength.

Erica, thank you for your meticulous proofreading and all the help you provided throughout this writing journey. Your contributions have elevated the quality of this book.

To my family and friends, both old and new, thank you for patiently listening to me talk about my dreams repeatedly and for offering your prayers, love, and support. Your belief in me has fueled my determination.

I am grateful to my writing coach, Michael, for making this dream a reality. Thank you for providing guidance, and encouragement, allowing me the space to ask for help when needed.

To my loyal dog, King, who always slept in the back of the room while I poured my heart into these pages. Thank you for reminding me to take breaks and play, even during the most challenging moments.

And lastly, to the readers of this book, I hope that my vulnerability and personal experiences will resonate with you and provide guidance and inspiration in navigating your own challenges.

Table of Contents

Section I: Introduction to Loss, Space, and Creation

Chapter 1: The Pain Point

I met him in college. I was a freshman around age 19. He was a year younger. He was a sophomore if memory serves me. I do remember that he lied about his age. After I viewed his birth certificate, he admitted later that he wanted to appear older, thinking I was only impressed with guys my age. Little did he know that his attentiveness and kindness were the traits that won me over.

He offered to carry my books while my arm was in a sling—an injury from the military where I had shoulder ligaments repaired. That is how he got my attention. He was good at showing up. Others came with offers, but he was always there. We became quick friends, often playing spades in the dorm lobby. We became great partners. He was the typical great catch: attentive, funny, tall, dark, and handsome.

I remember feeling that the campus in Fayetteville was not very safe. That's another great reason to have a friend around. But I wasn't willing to accept the risk anymore. I wanted to move back to Virginia. My boyfriend then said, "I'm coming with you."

My thoughts were more fairy tales than reality: *Wow. This is the real deal. He will leave North Carolina to be with me, not knowing anyone but me.* I felt the loyalty wash over me. He was serious about me.

My best friend had a place with a separate master suite. She welcomed us in. I attended business college in Harrisonburg. He went to work. Over the next year, we progressed to move into our place. That's when I found out I was pregnant.

The Pregnancy

I noticed my body changing quickly. I was peeing more than I should have for the quantity of water I was drinking. My friend flippantly asked if I was pregnant. I scoffed, "Because I'm peeing, I'm pregnant!" Disbelief and annoyance at her nerve for mentioning such a scandal.

"You could be. Let's take a test and see." Her pregnancy was already confirmed, her sister, my other best friend already had her baby. Our children would all be very close in age.

My boyfriend was at his friend's house when I shared the news with him. I told him that I took a pregnancy test, "The line is light. It may be positive, but I'm not sure." I told him this with indifference in my voice. I remember being nervous and wanting to know for sure. My best friend shared that her positive test was the same as mine (A very light line. My boyfriend asked me to come and get him.

"We need to get another test and confirm." He was excited.

When I found out I was pregnant at age 20, I questioned my next steps. I typically think in strategy rather than emotion.

First: Tell my best friend.

Second: Find prenatal care and read the books I need to read.

Third: Inform my parents.

I did not want my parents to find out another way. I don't remember how long I took to tell them, but it was soon after. They lived an hour and a half away. I called. I wanted to get it out of the way. I don't remember whether my boyfriend was there by my side. He was probably there.

We visited at some point, and my father said to my then-boyfriend, "You're going to marry her, right?" He was a man that believed in birthing babies within the confines of wedlock. My family, being Christian, was a template for my life. I also live my life for myself. That is my responsibility. I listen to the counsel and the wisdom of my upbringing, but I know I must make decisions for myself. The marriage conversation was an open conversation, not a mandate.

We told him that we had discussed marriage. I remember looking through books planning a marriage that we could afford. Dad offered to help with the wedding. He was significant in the process though he did not pay for all of it. My aunts were crafty. My cousin was our DJ. The wedding was held in our family church.

My Jordyn Da'yana

I don't remember being stressed. I had a huge belly and remembered often commenting that I was fat. I felt like a cliché getting married while pregnant. But I accepted that it was what it was. I was seven months pregnant as the wedding preparations were coming to fruition.

The pregnancy was difficult. I was attempting to keep up with school, walking, and eating right. One ultrasound pointed out that the baby had cystic hygroma. It looks like a pocket of fluid on the neck on the ultrasound. They told me that I would need a CVS (Chronic Villus Sample) test. The procedure requires that they take a piece of the placenta to test. It immediately makes the pregnancy high-risk. I was terrified that I would have a miscarriage. I had the test done. They told me that it was a boy with an extra chromosome. Klinesfelter syndrome was the diagnosis. I read up on how to support my baby. They kept asking me whether I wanted to terminate the pregnancy. I was not 16 weeks yet.

Weeks later, they performed another ultrasound. The technician asked whether I wanted to know the sex. "No. I had a CVS. I already know it is a boy." The look on her face was priceless. She went to get the genetics counselor. We looked and confirmed that it was a girl on the ultrasound. Confusion prevailed. And they continued to ask whether I wanted to terminate.

I woke up one day several weeks later and noticed my stomach was lopsided and I noticed she had not moved all day. I went to school thinking she was just sleeping. My baby was usually very active. I drank a glass of orange juice which normally got the baby moving. I left class early and went to the midwife I saw in Harrisonburg. My blood pressure was at a stroke level. The top number was over 200. They hooked me up and informed me that she wasn't breathing. Her heart was beating, but she was not breathing normally.

They rushed me to surgery. I was shaking. The nurse allowed me to wrap my arms around her while they did the spinal block. I had an irrational thought that they started the surgery too quickly before I became numb.

My husband could see everything. I talked to my husband, but I stopped breathing a few times. They coached me to continue breathing. I did not hear a sound when my daughter was born. I remember asking whether she was alive. I must have passed out. I awakened back in the hospital room. I was in and out of consciousness. I only remember a few family members who came to visit.

They did not have a NICU in this hospital, so Jordyn had to be transferred to UVA, which was an hour away. All of this threw me into chaos. I am methodical, a planner. In my birth plan, I had included a midwife and a warm bathtub to relax in. None of that happened. It certainly did not include me being separated from my child, not even knowing the sex or what the baby looked like. My plan did not mention me being incoherent and playing catch up on the whereabouts of my child.

My daughter was due in September; however, she came on 30 July, 9 days after I was married. My new husband and I were both 21. She was 3 lbs. It was an emergency C-section. It was traumatic for my new husband and me. I remember mainly because of a photo of my brother putting his hand up to the incubator. I remember she was just as big as his hand. I could not stop crying. We did not know what would happen to Jordyn or me. I was still at high risk myself. I named her Da'yana, which means Heavenly Divine. Her name came from wanting to give her the Jordyn (Jordan), my maiden name, knowing I was marrying and taking her father's name.

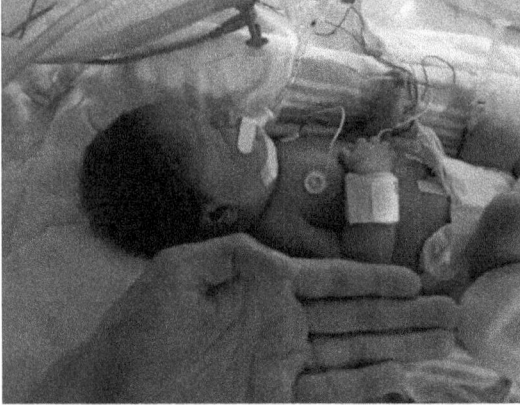

A Cloud Overhead

She was moved to UVA—an hour from Harrisonburg. I was only able to see her once before she was moved. I checked in on her regularly by phone, as I could not transfer with her. They kept calling her baby Jordyn rather than assigning a gender. That frustrated me. I wanted more information about my child. She had a mosaic trisomy 15 chromosome abnormality which is what they thought was a Y chromosome previously. No one could tell me what that meant. They were attempting to keep her stable. It took four days for me to get out of the hospital. My condition was not important to me. I remember losing a lot of blood when I stood up. My then-husband stated that I scarred him for life with the sight.

My nurse made me promise to call her with my blood pressure every couple of hours. That was her condition for allowing me to leave. I also promised I would go to the ER at UVA if needed.

I applied to the Ronald McDonald house down the street from UVA in Charlottesville, VA. We stayed there for a month. Baby Jordyn (she) was in the NICU. We were navigating a complex life right away.

When I finally saw her for only the second time, I was overcome but still aware of the surroundings. There was zero privacy in the NICU. The baby next to ours had a distended stomach and like Jordyn, his eyes were still closed due to swelling. When Jordyn finally opened her eyes, the mother next to us asked if she could share in the moment. I welcomed her. She seemed genuinely happy for us. She never saw her son open his eyes. He died within days of that moment. I still remember the look on her face as she shared it with us. I will never forget the experience of her pain. She was with us in the Ronald McDonald House. I knew her and her story. I witnessed her pain, unable to take her son home with her.

Jordyn was doing better and began to eat on her own. We moved to the next level. We stayed in the parenting suite, where they monitor parenting and caretaking. We passed all the tests and were cleared to take her home. We knew nothing more than that she was a preemie at that point.

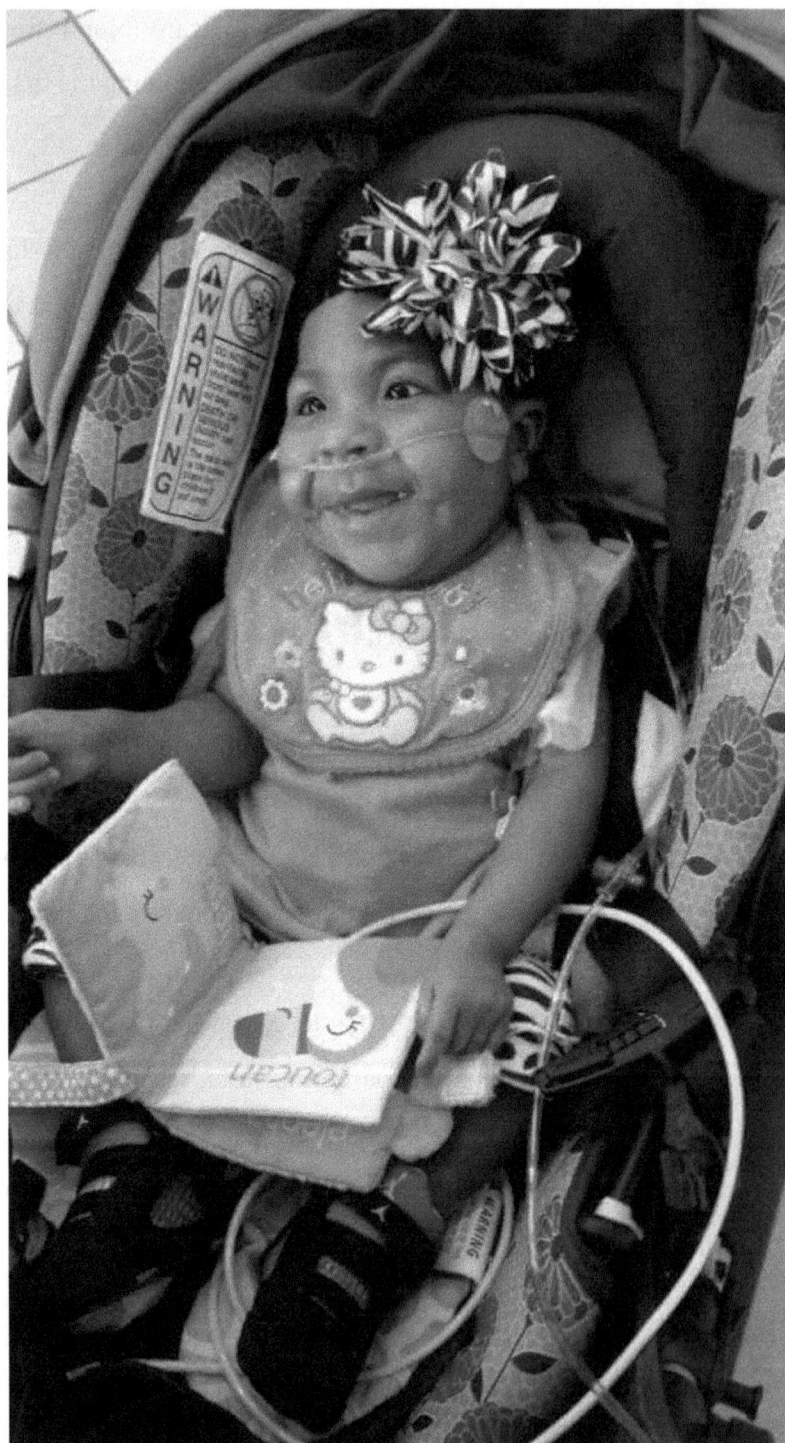

We found out that our daughter was terminally ill 3 months after she was born. My husband was supportive during that time. By the end of the next 9 months, my marriage was a very different experience. The once attentive man was now distant. I was often left by myself. He would decide to leave at critical moments without considering the family he was leaving behind.

I remember one pivotal moment when I complained to him, "If I am going to do everything myself, I will be by myself." After that, he left for an extended period.   Ten days later, my daughter died. I remember calling Jordyn's dad. I was empty and could not explain anything further. I asked the doctor to tell him what had occurred. The doctor complied. I asked him if he was coming. "For what?"

"We have a funeral to plan." I was still counting on him as if he had never left. He did not decline to assist with the funeral planning but said, "Call me if you need me." I chose not to call. The nastiness from his family is still visceral in my memory.

At the funeral, I invited him to the front row, his rightful place, because he truly loved his daughter, and she loved him regardless of our differences. Plus, there were good dad moments before. I recently spoke with him, and he talked about his journey of maturing. I wanted to make sure we recall the same things. He showed up for the funeral, but I realized that I did not need him for anything. I tried again to save our relationship and find what was once us. The loss had me searching for a connection.

Chapter 2: My Space

The act of creating space in our lives is a fundamental aspect of personal growth and fostering genuine connections with others. Some specific examples of how holding space can benefit others and lead to personal growth and fulfillment include:

Actively listening to a friend who is going through a difficult time, without offering unsolicited advice or judgment

Encouraging a colleague to share their thoughts and ideas in a meeting, creating an environment where everyone's input is valued.

Providing a safe space for a loved one to express their emotions and work through challenging experiences.

However, it is essential not to overlook the importance of creating space for ourselves as well. We can cultivate a more balanced and fulfilling life by setting aside time for self-reflection, self-care, and personal development. This balance allows us to be more present and effective when holding space for others, ultimately leading to deeper connections and a greater sense of well-being.

I remember an EMDR client that did not realize how much his childhood affected him. After it clicked one day in a session. "I never experienced love as a child. So, I never felt safe." It was a huge breakthrough for this client. That's how complex PTSD works. It is a complex combination of things. I used the float-back technique to explain to him the connection between childhood trauma and his current experiences. I explained that to heal and move forward, we must be vulnerable.

Vulnerability is not one of the courses we take in school. Especially coming out of the military or some other regimented life. You leave basic training after ten weeks and return to a world that has seemingly moved on without you. I remember the drill sergeants took our phones on day one and locked them up. We could only write letters to maintain a connection back home. Some recruits had gotten married right before or had plans right after. Some of us, like me, received a Dear John/Jane letter. The point is that you may need some assistance to reintegrate. The more profound point is that reintegration requires vulnerability. No one has trained us to be appropriate in our vulnerability.

Most of us put up walls that are boundaries to the extreme. They serve to keep people out, but they do not lend themselves to engagement, discernment, and communication. The installation of boundaries is a different consideration. Boundaries are lines that are not crossed but can have varying levels of permanence, allowing for engagement, discernment, and communication that are earned and continuously checked against impact, sustainability, and peace.

The Example Set

My mom was in an abusive relationship when I was 8-12. The experience was chaotic, and my sense of boundaries was skewed. One moment, my mother and stepfather were playful. The next, my stepfather was raging, and mom was stressed. I wanted to save my mother. I am not comfortable saying that she took his side, but she downplayed the danger and minimized his behavior, not wanting him to get into trouble even as the police were called.

I tried to make myself as small as possible. If they could not see me, if I were invisible, they would not challenge, reject, or dismiss me. I remember spending a lot of time in my room. Other than that, I don't remember much of my childhood. I remember the sense of inequity. Nothing seemed fair.

It took my mom years to catch on to the negative pattern. I found myself in a similar relationship but woke up within several months rather than years. I realized that my walls were not boundaries but tricks grief played on me.

2014 my daughter and my dad passed away. Then, a blank space. By the end of the year, I told myself, "You're too smart just to sit around." I moved from my hometown because my identity there was too tied to being "the young woman who lost her daughter." The town had rallied around me to raise money to cover her funeral expenses. I moved and was able to appreciate the loss as just part of my identity, not the whole.

I met a man while attending Delaware State. Things were going well in my life. I was getting good grades. I was moving forward. My life was looking good. That's how he got in. There were so many things that I ignored. I did not notice it at the time. He got through the protective walls I had put up. It led to me being pushed and shoved in uncomfortable directions.

I sat down one day and asked myself, "How in the world did you get here in this very toxic relationship." It clicked for me that if I got in this situation, I could get out. I feel for the people who cannot let go and see their way out. The grief was the emotional prison I sought to use for comfort. This man was my anchor to an improved life and experience. That was an inappropriate role for him. And he was not a good fit for the responsibility.

Learning appropriate vulnerability is a monumental task. I continue to learn that it is part of my journey and healing. I know that I have a great deal to learn. The goal is health. I am grateful I have a therapist to help me through it. I have a low tolerance for things that are not making me happy. My best friend makes my T-shirts, and one of the 13 characteristics on a shirt she made me is "Queen of Walking Away." Another best friend shared that it is a quality she admires due to my zero tolerance.

One thing that sticks out for me is being the only Black therapist in practice settings and other professional jobs I have held. I know now that I must show up and take up space. I can be who I am, change my hair, and engage authentically whether they are comfortable or not. My responses may put them on the defensive, but that is their baggage to hold in conversation, not mine. The representation of my presence as a Black woman gave comfort to so many. Clients requested me when they found out I was a Black therapist. They told me they were comforted and did not need to explain their anger and despair.

Boundaries by Henry Cloud

Unconditional love does not mean unconditional tolerance. Abuse, addiction, and other challenges are not tolerated in the name of unconditional love. I offer that you check in with yourself. Is the situation good for you? Does it make you happy? Check in with your sense of the present. Consult your value and your worth. Consider your voice and your options for addressing your emotional well-being.

You are never stuck. Take inventory of your situation. For example, the first questions in couples therapy explore commitment, trust, and love between the two people. If either of those is a failure, the relationship has failed. You must explore what you want and what you need. You must examine the important things that make the relationship valuable. Most people do not recognize their autonomy. They just don't know it. They have a comfort zone with the chaos of their lives. I remember Cardi B said something about her husband during a concert I attended, "Yeah. He cheats, but what am I going to do? Get with another man that cheats on me?" Tolerance is one thing, but the tacit acceptance of the reality that chaos is inevitable is the core problem. This is detrimental to your health.

I recognized that accepting and seeing the good side of people worked for my profession, but it does not work for life and romantic relationships. As a trained therapist, I hold space for people, but I am learning to do that less outside my work.

Learning is the critical element. You must want better with the expectations that there IS better. You will need to change the things that you put into your brain. Entertainment glorifies chaos and drama. There is no story without drama. But a healthy life is about peace and well-being. If you have never known peace, you may think that the content that you are consuming is normal and indifferent to your well-being. Your diet of media content and lifestyles impacts your experience. If you don't have an experience of healthy relationships, you can learn about it. Check it out on YouTube, TikTok, books, etc. (from a credible source, of course).

I remember a client that had a stalker relationship with a person that called her incessantly. When she entered a new relationship, she complained that the suitor did not call her enough. It took about two months of work to help her see that the chaos she was used to did not serve her well-being. The new experience was healthy; she found the "Aha Moment" through understanding attachment styles.

It allowed her to understand and choose the style that they resonated with most. She chose and began to understand what her style looked like, recognizing green flags and realistic expectations in the context of emotional awareness with the goal of creating secure attachments.

Creating a New Space

I have developed the position that I will check in with me daily. I created a space for ME without judgment. I also seek my own therapy to deal with what I need to work on. Boundaries are important because you must not be too kind to the point you get stepped on or taken advantage of. You must stand up for yourself. That may mean breaking a connection that you never wanted to break. I don't waste a lot of time. I create distance from the things that do not serve me. I evaluate things, check in with myself, and check the facts. If it does not serve a good purpose, I remove it.

Nonjudgement is the critical first element of a healthy space. "When I watch a sunset, I consider its beauty. I don't critique or criticize." It is what it is. You are simply looking at the situation's facts/evidence/reality. No interpretations or analyses, just the facts. DBT (Dialectic Behavior Therapy) has a concept of radical acceptance. It lessens the pain and anxiety of the equation. You accept the situation and how you feel about it, but you don't dwell on the chaos of it. You can move from the chaos into how you will solve the problem. This is empowerment. Accepting your pain helps you not to avoid it. After you have visited with your pain you can understand it better. You don't need to move in with it. A quick visit for more understanding will do.

Try Parts Work by Richard Schwartz—Internal Family Systems. Look at your internal "Self." Your Self is doing the healing. Your "Self" is when you feel the most centered. Explore what it feels like for you to be centered. When you explore your world with the 8 Cs, you find your true self. Calmness, clarity, compassion, curiosity, confidence, courage, creativity, and connectedness are the lenses to view the self within. Explore how your parts got their job they are doing. Look at the behaviors you have and how you feel about your reactions. The disconnect between your behavior and what you feel about yourself can be an opportunity to look at yourself in a way you never have before.

For example, have you ever noticed a behavior like Rage after you've been hurt? One of your exiled parts has been hurt, and Rage is here to extinguish the fire. You may also observe that when Rage enters, it creates more problems for you, so it is not helpful. You can explore Rage to understand better how to calm yourself to a more appropriate level. You may be able to create the space for a new experience and expression of self that is more consistent with who you are.

Section II: Holding Space for You

Chapter 3: Just Do It

When I joined the military, I learned you can "do it scared." No matter what is going on, for example, starting/ending a relationship is scary. Do it scared. Taking a solo trip can be very scary. Do it scared. Setting boundaries can be scary. Do it scared.

Sometimes you don't feel like it, but you must do it anyway. Even getting out of bed. You may not want to, but you have things to do.

NIC at Night (Night Infiltration Course): If you don't know what this is, it is an obstacle course several hundred meters on a low crawl through the sand. By the way, you are wearing full battle gear and are tasked with crawling with your rifle. Barbed wire overhead in some spurts. Fog of war in the darkness. And live rounds are being fired overhead, hearing grenades and mortars in the background. All I felt was fear. The tracer rounds looked like lasers; they would fall on the ground near me as I moved forward.

A shell got into my shirt and began to burn. I panicked. I thought I had been shot. I could see the ambulances arriving at the end. I froze for a moment. I immediately thought that the first responders were there for me. I was paralyzed with fear, certain that this is what it is like to be shot.

A drill sergeant saw me. I did not know that they were on the course with us. He began to yell orders, but they did not seem threatening. They were motivating. He motivated me to keep moving. It was a pep talk through yelling, but it worked. Every time I wanted to quit; I heard his voice.

I finally got to the end. The ambulance was not for me. This was the beginning of doing it scared. The next day while standing in formation, the drill sergeant took off his combat flag and told me to wear it for the day. "Private Jordan had to fight through some things last night. One of our Army values is Personal Courage. Last night, Jordan exemplified personal courage." While pregnant several years later, I had a vivid dream and woke up screaming, thinking I was shot again.

Military Experience

I was fresh out of high school in my first college experience. At age 16 I did not have the discipline to attend classes regularly. My mom and I were butting heads. The picture was painted that my father was not a living option. The process of joining the Army was quick because the ASVAP (The Armed Services Vocational Aptitude Battery) was available in my high school, allowing me to miss class for a couple of periods. I received a good score even though I only wanted to get out of class.

I was not happy with my home life. I was working at McDonald's on a work permit. I did not know what to do with my life. I drove 20 minutes to the Army recruiter's office. I told him what was going on at home. I thought about emancipation but that was not going to be a quick option. I wanted to be 18 so bad. I went with a friend who was supposed to enlist with me. My recruiter seemed to know that my friend would flake out. "If she doesn't come, are you still going to enlist?"

"She's coming. Don't worry."

"No. I am asking you for real. Are you still interested in leaving?"

"Yes. How soon can I get on the road?" It was less than 3 weeks before I was in basic training. After graduation, I was back in Virginia for job training- culinary school.

I remember talking to my dad, who was a Navy Vietnam veteran. I told him that I did not want to be in the city any longer. His response was, "The military is no place for a woman." I took that to mean that I could not do it. I saw it as a challenge. That is not how he meant it at all.

I soon found out that sexual assault, physical demands, and toxicity is not made for sensitivity, softness, and femininity. I often felt like an animal. For example, I got six vaccination shots almost at once. Immediately afterward, they told us to drop to the push-up position with our arms weak. Standard entrance week treatment.

I called my father on the one 5-minute phone call we had for the next few weeks and cried. "What did I do?"

"I tried to tell you. All you could do from this moment is complete it." So, I did.

What the Military Taught

My thoughts about the military are centered around discipline and financial security. But I also learned to stand up for myself. I had to post an equal opportunity complaint against a sergeant that I liked. In addition to the other things I endured, hearing the N-word was something I could not endure. Of course, you learn to respect your peers in the military. Yet, no one seemed to have empathy with me while I was pregnant. I learned that everyone was not my friend. I had to choose me first for the life of my baby.

In 2010, I tore the main ligaments of my shoulder. I was on a mobile kitchen trailer. The doctor I saw in Nevada told me it was tendonitis. They gave me a cortisone shot and told me it would be okay. It would not be okay. On the next physical examination, I was deemed unfit for duty. My first thought was to fight it so I could stay in. But I hated it and the racism I endured. I wanted to leave. I needed shoulder surgery, and my unit did not want to authorize it. I wrote to the governor and received credit repair as well as medical treatment. After that was resolved, I ran into complications with my pregnancy two years later and then later tried to return to duty. In 2012 I was breastfeeding and trying to attend as many drills as possible during this time.

2014 after losing my daughter, I found a recruiter that promised he could help. "Help me. But I don't want to be a culinary specialist any longer. Put me in HR." I went to him, sharing the full story of my experiences up to that point. He nodded as he leaned forward, seemingly connected to my every word. He reviewed my records and found that my shoulder needed evaluation before he could send me to admin training. Before he could complete my revision, he received orders to move to California and stuck me in a new unit as a culinary specialist like I asked him NOT to do.

It was 2015. Having not heard from the recruiter with any confirmation, I moved to Delaware State for my psychology degree. I sought meaning through all the loss I had experienced. By that May, I got a call from a Sergeant. I thought someone was playing on my phone. Fort Belvoir was calling to ask why I had not attended any drills. I did not know what he was talking about. I showed up the next month. The recruiter had a contract for a culinary specialist for 4 years that I had signed, thinking he was going to put me in an admin position! The sergeant initially did not believe me or work with me at all.

I was mortified that people thought I was Ms. Can't Get Right. I was also impressed by the Black leadership. The kitchen was not functional when I got there. I was tasked with getting the orders together for the kitchen. It was set in just a few months. That enabled them to see me for what and who I was, a hard-working woman of integrity. I began to see a new light as a leader in a healthy environment.

After a about a year my medical packet magically appears from my old unit from 2010 to complete my medical discharge. It was in

2017 that I was medically discharged. I was doing good work and progressing, but the medical packet deemed it was time to go.

Finishing School

At 16, I graduated high school and attended community college. I thought I wanted to be a certified nursing assistant. At the clinical, I found that it was something I did not want. I attended Saint Augustines in Raleigh to be an elementary school teacher. Next was Fayetteville State University to be a secondary school teacher. My dad drove me there, thinking that I would complete there. Colorado Technical University was where I got my associates in business administration. Delaware State is where I completed my bachelors in psychology. Then Walden University for my masters in clinical mental health counseling and doctorate in counselor education and supervision.

From 2008 to 2017, I was in the Army Reserves. I had a small break for a few months in 2013 because I lost my daughter. I would miss drills for those months around that time. I wrote to ask for an inactive designation to be placed in the inactive ready reserves. I wanted to spend time with my daughter, knowing she had a terminal illness. My daughter passed away that January 29[th, 2014]. I was in the back of the room working on my degree. I finally finished before my father's passing in April 2014. I was able to show my dad that I completed it. He could not talk at the time. He gave me a solid smile.

In the Spring of 2015, I started my bachelor's degree. I proposed that even if I hated it, I would complete it. I finished a year later in December 2016. Any completion is a win for me. From there, pursuing my master's degree was relatively without incident. I chose the school and program that was right for me. I am currently in my Doctoral program working through the process like a knife through butter— butter that I'm waiting to soften, but butter, nonetheless.

Chapter 4: Create Your Life

Create the life that you want, and don't waste time. If you had asked me about wasting time years ago, I might have given you a different answer. I may have talked about times when I did not know what to do—time I spent in the CNA program. I may have talked about relationships that I have endured. Today, I know that those experiences helped me become who I am. I don't think any of that time was a waste.

Fear

I talked to a client who asked about a decision, "What if I don't like it?"

"You may not. That's a part of living your life—finding out what you like and do not like." They were considering quitting their college studies. Fear was strong for them. I asked if they had a plan for something else. They had none. I asked, "What if you quit and find out after a couple of months that it is something you like?"

"I would regret it. I would feel bad that I could have been further along."

"That's your answer."

When I started college, I did not know what I wanted to do. I was 16. I was not disciplined. If you don't follow through and show up for class, you will not pass. From there, I attended different schools. I changed programs. I took my time. I figured it out and landed where I needed to be. You must be willing to succeed, but you must also be willing to fail as well.

This client is an OCD client. I worked to show them that they needed to expose themselves to things rather than avoid experiences. These exposures as baby steps are huge in the process.

I often use anxiety as an example. If a grizzly bear is in the room, we want anxiety. We need that feeling to get us moving. If we are trying new food and we feel the same anxiety, that is something that we need to check against what is appropriate. That feeling must be explored to see where it comes from.

I also think of teaching your brain. If you have learned that new things are scary and foreboding, you must train your brain to understand that calm is another option. Calm itself may be anxiety-producing, but practice will make perfect. Your nervous system is activated when it does not need to be activated. It has informed you over time that this thing is dangerous. Speak back to your brain and say, "I know you told me this is dangerous. I have evidence in the here and now that it is not. I will face the fear and assure myself that this is okay."

If someone comes in with bad anxiety and says, "I am going to pass out." I give them permission.'

"Okay. Pass out." That permission gives them an example. When they don't pass out, they have evidence that their fear is not warranted.

Evidence

Radical acceptance is my go-to when clients don't accept the realities they face. I remember a comparison picture I saw online. The image is of rain with a header stating, "It's raining." Two captions split the screen. On one side of the rain image, the caption says in response to the "It's raining" heading, "It's gloomy. I don't have the motivation." The other side says, "Yep." This is radical acceptance.

what is acceptance?

IT'S RAINING

i don't like rain.
i wish it wasn't raining.
my day would be better
if it wasn't raining. my day is
ruined. every day is like this.
it's always like this. why does
it always rain when all i want is
for it to be sunny?

IT'S RAINING

yup.

You can unlock the barrier to explore the present solutions rather than the experience you don't like. Radical acceptance allows you to move forward with your day. You may not like the rain, but you accept it, making it a less emotional experience. Radical acceptance is to cease to fight reality and stop destructive behaviors in response to what is real in your life.

Imagine yourself as a glass person. You shatter due to a tragedy. When you are picking up the pieces, you can take the pieces that work for you and rebuild yourself in a different way. You are never the same. You are different from that moment on. You can take only the pieces of yourself that you desire as you are rebuilding. You must figure out who you are now rather than living in the past. That is acceptable.

I liked that I was going to school, but I did not want to be a business major any longer. I wanted to focus on psychology. I honored the part of me that was driven to attend school. I integrated my new interest in the grief process, helping and engaging others in their pain.

There is nothing you can do to stop the rain. You acknowledge what is. That reduces your suffering. You refuse to allow reality to be processed as suffering. Once you can accept the situation in your life, you are able to move forward. You don't need to suffer. This does not mean that you like it. Things are painful. This is not "getting over it." This is acknowledging that you cannot control it. You decide to move beyond the barrier. Denying it as a barrier, accepting that it is a steppingstone. The "radical" in radical acceptance tells you that it is hard. It takes practice. With anything, persistent practice improves outcomes.

End of Suffering

In my doctoral program, we often discussed what theories, models, and techniques resonate with me. I am naturally person-centered. Everything else follows that. I fell in love with DBT and EMDR. In my life, there has been a lot of uncertainty. That supports anxiety.

When you learn radical acceptance, you must learn to keep the experiences from suffering. I lost my daughter. That pain can be excruciating. I must accept the reality and not live there stuck in bitterness, anger, and sadness because that is not beneficial to my life. I am not required to suffer because something bad happened to me.

The task is to make meaning out of grief. You have not gone through what you have gone through for nothing. I used to ask where my light was at the end of the tunnel. Someone responded, "Maybe you don't see the light because you are the light." That helped me so much. You are not going to see it if you are the light.

I found a group on Facebook, Alive Alone. I saw a post that I felt like commenting on. "Here's the truth about grief: loss gets integrated, not overcome. However long it takes, your heart and your mind will carve out a new life amid this weirdly devastated landscape. Little by little, pain and love will find ways to coexist." It's a quote by Megan Devine psychotherapist. My comment spurred multiple conversations about EMDR, which many respondents had not heard of. Many of them researched the technique and found therapists that could help them.

One commented, "You have surely heard this often, but you are an angel." I felt a sense of wow and wonder that my pain and integration could help another person.

I remember another person in my circle that wrote me a personal message. She shared that I am an inspiration. She said, "Know that someone is watching."

I remember the movie, Collateral Beauty. Will Smith's character loses his daughter, and the themes of love, time, and death are used to move him back to life. I was moved that the moments of loss can have beauty. I withdrew after my daughter's death. I continued to take my father to his doctor's appointments. I did not know that he had stage 4 cancer or that it would take him so rapidly. I lost him after losing my daughter, I shut down. I was out for at least eight months. That happens with complex grief.

I did not stay there. People have told me, "You can get rid of some of those baby things."

"I can. Or I could keep them as long as I want." I stood firm, holding my space. Yet, when a woman I knew had nothing for her child, I offered that she could come over and take what she wanted. That opportunity had that spontaneous, purposeful, meaningful element. I knew that my approach, sitting in my daughter's room and being stuck crying, was not helpful. I did not know what to do. There is no manual for losing a child to a rare heart disease with no cure (Pulmonary Vein Stenosis). I had to do what was good for me. I have given away clothes to a mother who had none, toys to my best friend's daycare, and books to mothers who read to their children.

While we lived in the hospital, I made sure she was dressed even if we walked to the rose garden or the cafeteria. The nurses would always comment on her 'best dressed" status. I made sure I kept her dressed. This was my joy. After she was gone, I found joy in offering another mother the chance to experience that same joy of dressing her daughter.

I have moved about 4 times since Jordyn left. I continue to move with that box of her things. I don't know what is in the box other than some toys. I am not ready to get rid of them. I hold that space for her. I may maintain some things that have dried out or that have become raggedy, but I'll go through them one day when I am ready. I cherish things like the bead necklace I made to commemorate the therapy, procedures, hospital admissions, and even sitting by the fish tank. The beads are all unique to time, place, and activity. I wanted it to be hers when she was older. It is now something that I will never let go of.

Chapter 5: Hold Space for You

Holding space describes the safe area for discussing your inner thoughts free of judgment. We talk about things in my therapy sessions that people don't talk about every day. I know it helps. I can help many people through their pain. But this is also a skill for You to do for You.

Judgment is the critical element to remove. Judgment happens in multiple ways. It can be a desire to fix or resolve the issue. A safe space is what people need for long-term help. If you go to a therapist for an intake, one very important factor is that you feel safe. I met a black woman searching for a woman of color as a therapist. She has relationship concerns and a plan to be married. I completed the intake and found that she had multiple sexual traumas in the past. She attended a therapist in the past. That doesn't matter, but this therapist asked about what she was wearing. It did not matter what she was wearing.

It was horrifying to hear that the therapist asked those questions. What she took from that was that the assault was her fault. My approach was to create a space for her to heal. I did not ask her those blaming questions. I asked her how the session went afterward, and she revealed that her presentation was a test. I passed, and she shared that she was willing to tell more beyond this true story that other therapists had blamed her for.

Gentle and Authentic

In therapy there is a certain level of gentleness I have to extend to each of my clients. When they are struggling with something that feels like a revolving door, we have to talk about it in the most authentic way possible. Some of the challenges shared feel familiar because they are the same. I open myself to hearing my client's take on the experience. I let them know, "This conversation sounds familiar, like a conversation we had a few weeks ago." This statement allows them to connect to the event where we talked. "Is this the same or different?" The goal is to compare them and identify the differences this time around. The final question is, "What do you need?". That is the self-check to see what they really need to help themselves or the situation.

Exploration is crucial to the experience and process of healing. The gentle approach enables people to process the pain of the topic without the pain of the current interaction. The follow-up questions invite the client to reach conclusions consistent with their desires.

Validation is the first step toward creating a gentle and authentic space. I do this in my interactions as a model for my clients. Self-validation can be very powerful in the healing process. Mindfulness, awareness, including acceptance are validating. Your feelings and thoughts are valid. I remember a client that was in an unhealthy relationship. She was uncomfortable talking about it and laughed nervously. I asked her whether she thought that she deserved the treatment she was receiving. Her answer was, "No." I note that she must validate her wishes to support herself now and in the future.

Later, if she is mistreated, I may ask, "Earlier, you said that this was not what you deserved. Has that changed?" This question often prompts them to engage in awareness within the therapy space and determine what is happening inside themselves. This self-awareness is the DBT STOP method. Stop. Take a step back. Observe the situation and others. Proceed mindfully.

Celebrating accomplishments is my favorite experience with clients. After we work through some EMDR targets, clients can achieve peace—some for the first time. After months or weeks of engagement, they evidence progress. I enjoy pointing that out to them and ensuring they recognize and integrate that progress. I have a client who asked whether he can give my information out because people ask him what he is doing differently. I have another client who is saying "Yes" more. The result is multiple trips overseas doing what they love to do.

Take a Step Back

The situations, thoughts, and emotions are going to be intense. Our nervous systems are toward fight, flight, freeze, or fawn. Taking a step back allows us to regulate our emotions. Emotional regulation is another DBT skill. There is a healing power from stepping back. The action of stepping away primarily allows the tension and intensity to subside. Your "wise mind" can speak more than your "emotional mind."

The wise mind also comes from DBT. The other mind is the reasonable mind. It is driven by logic. Feelings drive the emotional mind. The wise mind is the space in between, balanced. The reactive emotional mind makes decisions based on impulse without thinking them through. The reasonable mind lacks empathy and desire. The balance is recognizing and respecting feelings and responding to them in a rational way.

Often, the origin of the experience is a person blowing up/acting out of character. Taking a step back will often be applied after the blow-up. Our parts have triggers. It may be a child-rage part that is triggered. They rage. The other's child-binge part may be triggered. They go off to binge eat.

The more you know yourself and understand where this trauma response began, the closer you are to finding the need. You can turn inward and find that the child part of you needs a hug. You can imagine yourself hugging your inner child. You can then recognize the trigger and sort through that.

Ask, "What triggered me? Why did I blow up so bad?" The internal discussion covers self-knowledge and allows you to engage with the triggered part of yourself more healthily. An internal check is warranted and should be done often. Therapy can help. Reactions can exceed the situation and be based on trauma from your childhood that you only recognize because you had the blow-up.

The balance comes from accepting what you are used to. Your nervous system is trained on fight or flight. That will seem normal. You must recognize that you are comfortable with that response. You must intentionally choose to sit and have the conversation with the person that triggered you and within yourself.

Gottman and Coming Back for Repair

Repairing is explaining and asking for their take on the situation— precisely, the disagreement. The goal is to make statements that are connecting. Notice the difference between the following two statements:

"I am disappointed with you."
"I don't think either of us wanted to be in a misunderstanding."

The difference is that the first statement ends with placing blame even while opening to feel. This beginning may immediately doom the connection placing the other person on the defensive. Recognize that you may also be triggering the person because they may have a need based on wanting never to disappoint another person. This need may mean that the word triggers a disproportionate response from them.

Now, the stage is set for chaos and monologues that neither party hears from the other.

The second statement is an acknowledgment of feeling without judgment or placement of blame. It does not even address the original action. It instead focuses on the outcome, the experience felt by both parties. With this beginning, both parties can agree or disagree with the feeling and clarify as needed. Such an approach may allow reflection upon what the trigger was and how it may have little to do with the person. It may have everything to do with a past need that must be met.

Gottman's work and his Gottman Institute spent a great deal of time working out the language of dealing with triggers. He promotes a guide to coming back. It includes statements that return to the conversation with quotes that work in interactions. This is critical because the language in these moments can make or break the interaction. Poor communication creates more significant differences and triggers additional hurt between the parties involved.

Some of my favorites deal with expressing, returning, and addressing the trigger. See the following:

What Triggered Me?	Address the Trigger
"I felt excluded."	"Please say that more gently."
"I felt powerless."	"Please be quiet and listen to me."

What Triggered Me?	Address the Trigger
"I felt unheard."	"Give me a moment. I'll be back."
"I felt judged."	"Tell me what you hear me saying."
"I felt blamed."	"Let's compromise here."
"I felt a lack of passion."	"I see your point."
"I felt controlled."	"I know this isn't your fault."

The example wording is critical to your process of creating space. Many people often need help with the words in repairing after a blow-up or repairing a safe space. Questions of whether you like the other and engage in clarifying the blow-up, repairing the space. Sometimes there are bridges of humor or checking in that attempt to get to a position of repair. These are okay as they lead to additional clarifying dialogue.

Chapter 6: Prioritize Human Connection

We all have some experience that reminds us of our need for connection. Human connection is a basic need. The challenge is to connect with other humans in sustainable, mutually beneficial, and sober ways. These are the parameters of healthy relationships.

Sustainability. Thinking through what I have learned, I must not settle. There will be ups and downs in dealing with humans. You must get what you need. Discern by the actions of others, not the words alone. Sustainability, simply put, is knowing what you need and receiving it. More deeply, it is discerning whether what you want is truly what you need—whether it nurtures and supports your growth and development. No matter how constructed, your relationships must keep you moving forward in what you consider success. Otherwise, limit or cut them.

Mutually beneficial does not always mean that the relationships are reciprocal or 50/50. Sometimes the benefit is intangible on one side while tangible on the other. Sometimes, the transaction is 40/60 or some other combination. The point is that the relationship must be satisfying and agreeable to both parties. With that foundation, progress can be made.

Sobriety is perhaps the most difficult of the healthy relationship parameters. We can sometimes get so enamored with the superficial aspects of the relationship that we do not take the time to see the deeper meanings, intentions, fallacies, and deficits the interactions demonstrate. We can be "Drunk in Love," to quote a famous song phrase. The critical exercise is identifying where your acceptance of problem relationships comes from. Maybe you want to make peace, be better, resist thinking you're perfect, or some other growth process. You must not allow the deficits of others and the damage they perpetuate within relationships because you are still working on yourself. Maintain a healthy standard (not perfection) even while you recognize your unhealthy traits and work to address them healthily. Refuse the tendency to allow someone to mistreat you because they apologize and remind you of your faults. "Nobody's perfect" is not a license to accept a cycle of abuse.

I suggest at least four techniques for engaging effectively with human connections. You will notice that each is an approach to you that extends to the others. Beginning with you is the only way to gain in human interactions. You are the only thing you can control, and even then, your perceived control is only an ability to respond intentionally to your neuro-biochemical-emotional triggers.

Checking In with You

Having family, friends, and your circle is excellent, but you must live with yourself at the end of the day. Know what you are okay with. I am a therapist—a student of human behavior and an expert on holding space. I must still check in with myself. I am not immune to the need for clarity, accountability, and reflection.

Immediately after an altercation, you can give yourself a pause so that you may self-reflect. You have some blind spots that you must work on or integrate. Your initial review may confirm that you did nothing wrong. Your after-action report may look at what happened, what went well, and what can be improved. Sometimes, the problem is you.

When you check in with yourself, you must be critically honest. You know what you are doing and how you are living. A therapist will be honest with you, but they review from the outside. Seeking therapy can provide a sounding board for you. An objective voice can give you a mirror to see yourself more clearly. Often, you find that the things you may have thought you were over continuing as triggers. The benefit of therapy is that you can work through that with a professional.

Deal Breakers

Know your deal breakers. The first question is a question of tolerance. The challenge is to understand that many have continued in relationships through their deal breakers. You can idealize and fantasize, but practice living specifically in the moment. I remember a client in a long-distance relationship. Every time the friend is supposed to move, his father guilt trips that he will die if the friend moves. I inquired about the duration of the injury. I inquired about the feelings and whether there was resentment forming. "Honestly, I am getting tired of it. But I am tired of dating."

"How does that impact your mental health as you deal with this?"

Those honest discussions are critical to your decision-making. They indicate that the boundary is being crossed.

The critical reflection is to examine your part in every interaction. One thing that is not okay may happen, and you may launch into all the things that are not okay. One incident can become a tremendous experience of hurt and response to trauma. Your prior trauma can resurface with a tendency of most of us to blame others or unreasonably require others to shoulder our trauma. You may be placing the responsibility for your triggers on others. This is especially important when you have not shared your trauma, process, and healing journey with another person.

Accountability

Hold yourself accountable. I remember the moment when I decided to leave a previous relationship. I looked in the mirror and asked myself, "Who are you?" I realized that I had lost myself in the relationship.

The cycle starts subtly with some loss or insecurity that questions your contribution. Over time, you ask yourself questions about your role and whether you have given enough of yourself. That question is potentially damaging because you must know what your limits are, so you don't give and give until there isn't any more to give. Give your best every day, it is all you can do. Once you have given your best, never question how another person perceives that best. Never allow someone to question your best. You are not called to change the involvement of another. Share your need if it is not being met. You must be willing to have some difficult conversations.

The other person in your interactions must be accountable for their actions. You ask yourself whether you can meet this person where they are or whether you must call it quits. If you can provide time and space, express true feelings in service to reparation, and focus on progress in your individual development, the relationship may be worth repairing. Back to the personal check-in, you can confirm whether the healing feels genuine.

Accept Failure

Another important consideration is not being afraid to change your mind or fail. You can be head over heels, but if someone treats you poorly or if the relationship doesn't serve you, you can let it go. You are the center of your world. The connection is not. You will never lose yourself if you maintain yourself as the center. They are not to be the center. They can be an extension. If they go away, you are not lost.

I remember the mirror being held to me when my best friend told me about intimate partner violence in her relationship. I thought, *how can I say anything to her when I am sitting here putting up with what I am putting up with?* Some people are on their high horse and feel they cannot be checked. Your check-in must include self-awareness of the potential for failure, disappointment, and incompatibility. These are not pessimistic but realistic. They keep you in a position to be authentic, aware, and responsive as a healthy engagement in every human interaction.

Chapter 7: Validate Your Feelings

Whatever hurts for you is valid and deserves to be attended to. If people affect me in a negative way, I must distance myself from them. I have practiced deepening my awareness, giving myself space to make my observations, and accepting the reality before me. It begins with acknowledgment, acceptance, then understanding, that equals self-validation. Emotions are all about expression. More specifically, it is a shaking and shifting of the feelings you have based on your experiences. I love that part of Kirk Franklin's song Declaration, "I'm going to cry now and get it out of my system." You must listen to your emotions and feel them to heal them.

When I heard it, I replied, "This is it." When letting go and validating your feelings, you are letting go of the trauma from your nervous system. I remember a client who was having a grief attack. He attempted to gloss over it and move on. I stopped him for pause. I asked one question, and he immediately began to cry. He was able to unpack some of the feelings, acknowledge them, and give himself permission to grieve. He felt better after a moment.

You will have these moments. When you hold them in by glossing over them, they get worse and set up shop in your body. You don't have to move in, but you can visit them. Fall apart for that moment. Put yourself back together with the pieces you want to take. The Franklin song also says, "Can't be here next year, giving these same tears." Yes. Release it. Grow. Heal.

Awareness. I saw a Tik-Tok the other day that brought it home for me. He asked, "What would you do if no one chose to marry you?" I thought about the question. I laughed. I would be doing the same thing. I would live my best life. I would still be the best therapist I could be. I would spend time with family, travel, and continue to help people. People often want to have the American dream of family, children, and a home. I had these at one time. My daughter passed away. My husband and I divorced. I had a halt in my life. I had to piece it back together.

In a sense, we are all always doing that. I had to learn what being alone looks like for me. I know now that it is peace and happiness for me. When I moved into my new house, I purchased new furniture without having to consult another person. It is girly furniture with diamonds in it, unapologetically. I am learning to have fun with that freedom. You can enjoy freedom if you are open to it.

I love the idea of a perfect fit—the person for you will just fit without compromise. But I don't know if I truly believe that. I am still figuring it out. You know the green relationship flags: empathy, honoring the relationship, self-sufficiency, and more. You also know the red flags. How many do you accept or even acknowledge?

The question of awareness is centered on what the relationship adds to your life. You live all your life with yourself with or without the absence of others. I get deep into the emotions of the hard realities people deal with every day. I am often drained. If my person cannot contribute to a peaceful experience and engage in that space with me for development, they must go.

Mindfulness is knowing and being aware of yourself. When I feel good about my day, the feeling remains. I must consistently explore and understand my origins, preferences, and interpretations. Consider self-development to be a necessity. My suggestion will always be to seek therapy for extra support in self-development. Alternatively, you can look for books that can educate you on any questions and explorations you find to be without, from a credible source, of course.

Observations. They are neither good nor bad—no need to give them a label, they just are. I remember engaging with people who take me for granted in many aspects of life. I am still trying to figure out how to navigate these experiences. The bottom line is that each encounter is information.

I remember an episode of Married at First Sight. It was the meeting with the experts to decide whether they would stay married. If you don't know the show, two people are matched by experts and married at first sight. Eight weeks after their interactions, they choose whether to stay married. They get to learn all the features of their partner's personality.

I don't know if I like the show. It seems that there is a great deal of pressure to stay married. As a black woman, I am used to depictions of "struggle love." Too many examples of marrying people and having to struggle with infidelity, grief, or addictions. To be fair, I wonder aloud what we must overlook in another human being.

Your observations help to communicate the compromises that may work in the relationship. For example, if I am engaging with a person who prefers to text rather than talk, I can offer a conversation about whether there is a middle for us to meet.

Take note and engage in communication. There is a difference between issues that can be discussed and abuse. These lines must be communicated so that both parties are aware.

Acceptance. Allow them to be. It is okay if no one agrees with me. It is an interesting process of letting go of what others think. It must be learned because we all care about what others think.

I remember worrying about what others would think as I contemplated my second divorce. I knew it was an abusive relationship that made me miserable. I had to ask whether I would allow the view of others to hinder my actions. I am not giving up. I am accepting what is happening and what is the healthy response. I had to refuse the view of this choice as a weakness.

You must choose yourself first. The information is in your decision-making process but is not the determinant of my definition of self. I am not a weak person. It applies to the course of action, not my definition. It is not selfish to put yourself first. It is necessary.

This is reality right now. You are not required to like it. You must simply accept—stop fighting with it. Life is still worth living. You just need to figure it out. Your character speaks for itself. No matter who is debating you, talking about you, or speaking their truth about you, the evidence is what matters. For example, if I am being shamed for not cooking and cleaning, the posts on Instagram of all the meals I made speak for themselves. Even if there wasn't an Instagram, people are not the determinant of who you are.

You must be true to yourself. You need to sit with yourself and figure out what and who you are. If you don't, you risk molding yourself into the image of what others think rather than what you want for yourself. Let alone what God wants for you. He wants you to live life more abundantly. If that is not the reality, seek better.

Section III: Living Within Your Space

Chapter 8: Setting Yourself Up for Success

Fatality

You will go through life, and bad things will happen. You could be the best person in the world, and bad things still happen. Take the knife out of your heart and use it as a sword. Life has a level of messiness. But you can also protect yourself.

Life goes on whether we want it to or not. I adopted this phrase after I lost my daughter. Life continues to move forward. I asked myself, "Do you want life to go on miserably or better?" I wanted to take back my control. Some events are beyond our control. My loss was beyond my control. I could not accept that I would lose my first child. I would never have wanted that to happen.

What is within my control is putting one foot in front of the other. I can keep moving. My fate is not to be mediocre. I decided not to crawl through all this pain for nothing or live in that small space. Growth is not striving for perfection. We will never reach that. Life is striving for excellence. I think about making it happen—whatever IT is.

I remember wanting to write a book and searching for help to make it happen. I found that my goals have help available. I don't need to do everything myself. When you know better, you do better. I don't know when it changed for me, from doing it myself to getting help or accepting help. Even with my significant other, I find it hard to accept that he has taken over tasks and provided help. My father was like that. That's why I miss him so much. My mother is very independent. I still try not to need anything and solidify my independence but also accept help, I am trying to find my balance.

We create familiar comfort zones through what is beneficial for us. If you have few people to count on, you learn that independence (not asking for help) keeps you from feelings of rejection or perceptions of desperation. For me, avoidance is different from setting a boundary. Notice what you are doing in your interactions. If you look externally for validation, you are on a shaky path. Validation, motivation, and worth are best originated from the inside. You can find confirmation, inspiration, and value in others. What is most important is that you can also give them to yourself.

I know there are people I can go to for help and others in my circle that I cannot. For financial support, I know whom to go to. For emotional support, I know that others are better to ask when I need support. This learning is protecting oneself or avoiding mental and emotional stress. I know whom I can be vulnerable and authentic with. It is okay that you cannot be authentic and open with everyone.

Boundaries are different from avoidance or self-protection. They come in different categories: physical boundaries, emotional boundaries, time boundaries, sexual boundaries, intellectual boundaries, and material boundaries. Emotional, material, and intellectual boundaries are the ones I often help people through. As I think of my clients, physical and sexual boundaries are being violated due to obligation.

You must know how you use your time. My time is split between two jobs, finishing my Ph.D., housework, communication with family and friends, running a business, content creation, and self-care. I also maintain a romantic relationship. I must create time boundaries. I feel better when I connect these boundaries with my goals. Boundaries can be violated when someone demands more of my time than I am willing to give. If I am not firm and accept that violation, the stressors will be ever-present. The process is to set the boundary, monitor the boundary, and communicate the violation when boundaries are violated.

Healthy Relationships

Resisting the super-damaged person is critical, especially for natural empaths, helpers, and every codependent person. Most of us understand how to grieve, but I question whether we truly know how to heal. Once we survive, do we know how to intentionally thrive?

People come into your life with their experiences, needs, and developments. Your task is to evaluate their compatibility with your lifestyle. I think of the person who begins a relationship by always calling and checking up on you. In the beginning, you think of the behavior as sweet. You are thankful that they are concerned about your health and well-being. You get used to being on call and accessible to this other person.

As time passes, your perception of health and well-being checks reveals tracking behavior and possessiveness. Often, only after the relationship do you realize that the behavior was toxic. They were not concerned about you. They were concerned about where you were and what you were doing. The check-in was not in service of you. It was in service of their own needs for validation.

In the next relationship, you may transfer the learning that calling and checking in often is appropriate. You may fault a new person for not checking in as much as you are used to. This could cause conflict because the other misunderstands your reasoning for the ask. You must re-learn what is appropriate based on your self-knowledge and your set of boundaries. Resist the inclination to use the last relationship as a basis for new interactions. Use yourself and secure attachment as the standard, and engage in a standard based on health, reason, and sustainability.

I can change the unsustainable learning and unlearn. Yesterday's Arielle is not today's Arielle. If there are behaviors in my past that were toxic, I must strive to do better and accept better, not repeat the cycle.

The question is: How do I get my needs met without needing so much external validation? Knowing yourself is a critical element of health and secure attachment. If a person monopolizes your time, you cannot engage in self-reflection and self-development. You may sense the discomfort, but it is crucial to continued development. Flexibility is another component. You may not have all the answers. Continued growth is another vital experience. You are learning and growing every day. You can find new questions and explore new answers daily.

Boundaries can help to rule out incompatibility and confirm relationships that have growth potential. You can't change a person into what you want them to be. Resist trying. We often do this to validate ourselves as healers and "good people." But this is an unhealthy way to validate your sense of self. This dis-ease works both ways. A lack of self-knowledge can cause you to be shaped into an image the other person presents. The result will always be hurt feelings and possibly betrayal when your true self gains the courage to surface.

I remember being asked in dating interactions, "What are you looking for in a man?"

"Why, so you can pretend to be that? Why don't you tell me who you are, and we can move from there." Some may have thought that I was being harsh or aggressive, but I was maintaining the boundary—a primary boundary—to express self rather than to mold self, motivated by attraction. I held that boundary, knowing healthy partnership relationships are about compatibility along with compromise. The better each person is at setting, monitoring, and communicating, the better the experience and outcomes of the relationship.

Moreover, most people can only pretend for 90 days or less. I have had these experiences where I would tell what I desired in a partner. The person would act accordingly until they could not pretend any longer. Each of those interactions ended hurtfully. When you have done everything and been open and honest with another person, their deceit hits your core. You are writing a piece of reciprocity while the person is not on the same page.

Thriving Defined

Thriving is progressively improving health and well-being through self-expression. My thriving experience can be distilled into a set of principles for recognizing that you need help—that no one successfully does life alone. Though we often discuss romantic relationships in these discussions, the foundation of thriving is not romantic relationships. Supportive relationships are the foundation. Therefore, many states that, in romance, they want friendship first.

The friendship they describe is a supportive relationship that begins with self-knowledge on the part of both parties, progressive interactions, and open communication. With complementary skill sets, these friends can accomplish more than alone. They find an outlet for their creative expression and a boost to their internal validation, motivation, and worth from external confirmation, inspiration, and value.

Boundaries protect you in the context of what you know about yourself, what you contribute to interactions, and what you are willing to tolerate. You can mess up, but how do you repair it? Boundaries are most discussed when they are violated.

A suitable apology is not just words; it is an action as an expression of character. Expressions of character are loyalty to my boundaries. More than just flowers after an argument or tears, heartfelt apologies are corrections of behavior and respect for boundaries as they are presented.

So, what if the steps toward managing our boundaries are principles for thriving? If they were (which they are), they would be expressed as follows:

Set Boundaries. Explore yourself. Express yourself. Determine what circumstances and interactions offer safe space for you to present, affirm, examine, and correct your expression. Determine compatibility between you and others based on your boundaries as character expressions. Conceptualize multiple levels of accessibility—circles of influence around you. Allow people to exit inner circles and move outward based on incompatibility.

Monitor Boundaries. Be impeccable with your word and your boundaries. If you have set a boundary, require others to adhere to it. If they are not willing, allow them to exit. When violations occur, not the reasoning employed testing it against your sense of fairness, empathy, and sustainability. Their perception may offer a new perspective you would do well to consider. Or it could be confirmation that the two of you do not complement each other.

Communicate. The violation is only part of the problem. The repair after they violate the boundary is critical. Do not move the boundary or negotiate. Your boundary is vital to your success. You must be willing to communicate. These are not only corrective interactions. They are the foundation for growth and development that are the benefit of relationships. Communication addresses misunderstandings, and it clarifies boundaries of all types.

Chapter 9: Relationships Within Your Space

Love, Empathy, and Sitting with Your Feelings

Imagine discovering love at an adult age. So many adults have not discovered the experience of true, unconditional love. I chose the adult population because of my work with children. I needed the parents to reach out to engage and support the children. The central question is about who teaches this concept of real love. A lot of us don't come from an ideal family with a chance to learn and engage in genuine love.

I see the results in my work every day. The absence of experience with love and the detriments of trauma are evident. I engage to disarm and reframe resistance and defensiveness in sessions. Clients are uncomfortable and uncertain about being vulnerable. I attempt to make the burdens lighter and normalize the healing process for my clients. "There's that avoidance coming up." Self-reflection and mindfulness are critical to the process.

You must break the cycle of anxiety. Triggers lead to avoidance. Avoidance provides short-term relief but long-term anxiety. In response to the trigger, explore. Consider what you experience. Sitting with the trigger and the explanation opens your brain to find solutions. Avoidance robs your brain of the opportunity to help you.

I remember my interactions when sharing my experience of loss with people. After sharing the loss of my daughter, they would tear up, "Oh my! I am so sorry for your loss." I would end up attending to their sense of grief and their overwhelming empathy for me. I no longer do that.

I allow people to sit with their feelings. They are entitled to their response to the information and their preference in the interaction. My job is not to save them from their feelings, especially not knowing where their response originates. They may have similar experiences or fears. They may be highly empathetic. I don't know. I know that genuine emotional expression is the foundation of healthy relationships.

Avoidance is Like Lying to Yourself

You may avoid your fears. As a result, your fears grow. Some think of this as lying or being inauthentic. I see it more specifically as avoidance. It is seeking short-term relief. You may have experienced short-term relief, which is why you are avoidant.

Anxiety is helpful in extreme situations. For example, if a grizzly bear comes into the room, you must engage in fight or flight. But you must check if your brain is firing in response to normal situations. This is the mindfulness that redresses the situation and your experience.

I have a client that prefaces his statements with, "This may sound crazy, but...." I challenged him to think about why he makes those statements.

"I'm a therapist. Nothing sounds crazy to me. Do you realize that you are asking that question before your statements? Are you judging yourself? Do you think I will judge you?" He thought about it and will continue to consider it this week.

The challenge is critical to motivating the work of mindfulness, even in the cycle of relief. I remember a client that got into a relationship with a person. Shortly afterward, they determined that they did not want to be in a relationship with the person. They did not tell the person. They were avoiding the conversation because they were saving the other person's feelings. There is short-term relief, but life changes require addressing the situation as the relationship progresses. You still end up hurting their feelings. You still feel bad. The time, bond, and experience were longer, and the hurt multiplied.

You do no favors by hiding your true feelings. The internal conflict must be addressed, whether physical, mental, or spiritual. Explore those feelings and determine the core explanation or solution to your conflict. You must be able to name your feelings and explain your why. If you are clinching your fists or tensing up, feeling exhausted and anxious, or feeling hopeless, uninspired, or unmotivated, you must engage the why of those reactions. Your body will tell the story. Your mind will interpret.

Working Through Loss

Never allow yourself to be caught up in what you want another person to be. You must meet people where they are. So what if we are into session 10, and they have not made progress? Maybe it will be level 11 that they make progress. Check-in. "How do you feel about your progress up to this point?"

"I feel I am doing okay but want to make more."

This is the usual interaction. Most often, we are on the same page. I don't experience a lot of avoidance in this context. I put the responsibility on the client and encourage them to work harder than I am in attending to their goals. Another intervention or modality may be needed. I may need to explore their experience, childhood, or other profile factors. But, at its core, the challenge is my expectations.

This is an approach to yourself and well. Sometimes you work harder to meet expectations that are not truly valuable to your definition of self. I remember being frustrated about clients missing appointments. A conversation with a supervisor allowed me to separate my definition of how much I care from my definition of myself as a therapist.

"It doesn't reflect who you are as a therapist," were the words of my supervisor. I apply that to my life, attempting not to take things personally. Some things are personal, but I separate myself. "It doesn't reflect who I am as a person." I journal and release my feelings. This helps me organize my thoughts and select the appropriate action for the situation.

My father and baby passed within 3 months of each other. I changed my degree from business to psychology. Ultimately, I needed an adjustment in my expectation. I recognized my ability to create my reality rather than give myself over to fate and any expectation. This is a shift that becomes easier with feelings of anger and frustration. It is potentially slower with grief, but the potential for motivation is present.

What I saw in my life was the loss of Jordyn in January and the loss of my father in April. I fell apart. I don't remember those 8 months. Around my birthday in October, I was looking into a mirror (I don't know if it was figuratively or literally), but I heard, "You are too smart to sit around and waste away." I did not know what I would do in response to this. I knew I wanted to go back to school. I had been to several and was worried about completing. I said to myself, "There is no greater loss than losing your daughter and father. Whatever school I attend, I will finish." I explored many schools. I determined that an HBCU was the best fit for me. I moved into a room without a roommate even though it was more expensive. I had to map out how to engage the cafeteria, gym, and class because my anxiety was so high. After exposure, I became okay enough to branch out to speaking engagements, clubs, and other experiences.

I finished and kept putting one foot in front of another. I never envisioned working and achieving a master's degree. I remember feeling lonely during the virtual graduation without family. I purchased a balloon from the dollar store and sat in front of the screen. My next move to seek my doctoral degree connected because I saw an opportunity even in the aftermath of my experiences.

For me, it was normalizing the return. None of this stops me from missing my daughter each and every day. I still find that I don't want to participate in certain things around certain times. It is hard and harder at times. I allow myself to let it be hard in those times. Practicing gratitude helps during those hard times. I am grateful for the time that I did have with loved ones. Those times were incredibly special. I still want to share my accomplishments with my father. He would be so proud. Losing my child is a non-normative event that offers different challenges. My two best friends had children at the same time as me. I find myself wondering what my daughter would like, how she would get into trouble, and more. I keep her flower bow with me in my car. I keep a necklace of her handprint around my neck. These are the things that make me feel good. Do the things that make you feel good.

Chapter 10: Letting Go & Moving On

When I think about letting go and moving on, I think about many things: unwanted behaviors, unwanted people, and the magic of new beginnings. Ending is a good thing. They are necessary. We would be stuck if we did not end things. You can find endings throughout your life. They are the steppingstones to progress. They are what life is about. You cannot escape those.

I do not like when people say that I need to let go and move on from my grief. I don't conceptualize it that way. Often, these requests are an attempt by the stating person to make themselves feel better. The request is for them, not me. It is my choice to keep mementos and memories, even if they are emotion-laden. Life goes on whether you want it to or not. You make the choice whether you move on terribly and stuck or with purpose and intention. Being alive means that we are moving.

I have had people ask me how I am okay after the grief that initiated my quest for healing. I tell them that I cannot help, but I can only tell them what I have done. There is no survival guide for losing a child. I did not know what to do. The emotions were myriad: sadness, being frustrated for being so sad. No one around me understood. Even the closest person beside me, her dad, did not get it. I was her mother. That place is unique. I did not want sympathy. I could not escape the sad discussions, hugs, and being reminded of my grief through people's reactions.

My brother experienced something of loss during the same time. We ended up living together. It helped to be with someone who experienced something similar at the time. We were both just surviving, reminding each other to eat. It was a seasonal-type experience. We crawled, began to walk, and move forward. He visited colleges with me when I was exploring. After my revelation that I was too smart, he was the person I told. I don't remember a lot during those 8 months, but I remember the quality time we shared.

Life Stressors

I opened my part-time practice. I realized that working for people is for them. They want you to meet numbers for them. They are not concerned with your life and work. I wanted to go to Tahoe for a break. They told me I didn't have much time left. I was checking on my grandmother, advocating for my mom, and attending school.

I realized that I had not submitted a timesheet for a period at work. In August, my mother had a fall, was bussed home by ambulance, got blood clots in her legs, and declined rapidly. I reduced my workload at work to care for my mother. The engagement with the doctors has been worrisome, to say the least. I was there for my mother, advocating and providing care. Nothing else was important. I could not take as much as I was able to take prior. I started therapy, a new relationship, and this writing project around that time. I realized that I had other things to work on with my therapist. I never took the average of 25 clients per week. That made me an hourly employee…unbeknownst to me.

I cannot blame anyone for this new reality. The bottom line is that I must set myself up for success. No one else is going to do it. I am on the road to working for myself. It is scary, but I know I need to do it. Moreover, I know that it is something that I have always wanted to do. These are the stressors, but again, self-knowledge of your ability, your desires, and your options is critical.

I had a client that came into a session with the admonishment, "It's working!" He had gone out and did not have anxiety for the first time in his life. He was able to observe without pressure and tension. He expressed his gratitude that the process was working.

After our last session, he voiced the feeling that the EMDR feels like an identity crisis each time. The unlocking of the levels of self-awareness can be unsettling. You begin to process the trauma and connect with the inner children and the moments of resolution. You then are tasked to reintegrate the person you can be and are becoming. This can be truly unsettling, but that process is the process of living, growing, and progressing.

Your Power

The person that I married knew that I had been through a lot, then added more. Recognize your worth and move when you must. You may sit in misery without realizing the pain if you are conditioned for less than you deserve. During the aftermath of my loss and starting school, I began my divorce.

I was on a campus where no one knew me. I shed the identity of being the woman who lost her baby and her father. I made up my mind to complete my degree. I had no idea how much I enjoyed psychology and helping people with their struggles until I began my learning and internship. I started online for a Master's degree and finished before my cohort.

It was a great feeling to feel that I was on track even after all that I had been through. I completed that degree feeling that I learned more. I have continued as a lifelong learner. I was no longer a plant with its root dying on the inside. I am a healthy plant, free to expand in larger and larger pots to flourish.

A great revelation was to accept the power to stand up for myself and leave from relationships that do not feed me. I learned to enjoy my own company. After my second divorce, I got my yorkie. He's amazing. You can figure it out. You can figure out what you need and what makes you content.

I remember being triggered by a client who was combative. I asked how she was doing over the last two weeks. I know what her diagnosis is and how negative the call will be because of it. This particular day, she challenged me, "I notice that my other therapist is making more progress with me than you." She focused on her lack of progress. She accused me of typing. I was not. "I feel more comfortable with your hands up." She continued to sit with that while being combative. Our last session was target-mapping for the EMDR. I surmised that her comparison of me to the other therapist was her resistance to the opportunity (work) of the EMDR. The process is not going to be easy. She certainly was intuitive and defensive about the work.

If you want to stay in your place of depression, anger, and disappointment, you can stay there. No therapist or coach can help you to move when you are rooted in staying still. I still saw positives in the fact that she was choosing for herself. She has noted progress up to this point, but this day was different. She would not allow me to help. She was dysregulated that day. I sent her some DBT regulation tips after the session. I hope she practiced them.

She needed to center, release, and express what she needed. I think of this for myself. This is self-knowledge. I know that women wrestle with hormones and have trouble expressing themselves. The ideas can flow. You can try different things. Do something about it. This is your power.

Charming or Charmed

I married another charming guy whom I thought was a good partner. He began to flip the script. It was nice and refreshing after losing my father, marriage, and daughter. We dated for a year. We planned a wedding and married. On the wedding night, we had an argument and a physical altercation.

"You think you can put your hands on me?"

"You married me!"

"I didn't think it would be a punishment." Five months later, I strategically planned a move. The total relationship was around three years. I moved on a Friday and started work on that Monday. No one knew.

My move forward is not going to be stressful; I know. I have a system and procedure for doing what I need to do. Leaving the group practice and working for myself will be a truly good thing. What did it for me was the math. I simply calculated the money. I calculated the quality of life on the complex side. I went back to the phrase, "Just do it!" Don't do it maliciously or haphazardly, but just do it. Be smart about it but move when necessary.

I listened to a TikTok captioned, "You are Chosen." One of the things it said was that our ancestors completed their contribution, whether good or bad. You carry some of that energy forward as you live. If I take on that in the gift of healing, I can define myself as a trauma healer. I can take each client in stride whether they persist or leave treatment. Whether the client is complimentary or resistant, I never need to question who I am and my chosen status as a healer.

I have been told by clients, coworkers, and others, "You were born to do this." It is a nice thing to hear, AND it also speaks to the work that I have done with my gift. I have always been the "watch me" type.

They say I won't get a job with a bachelor's degree in psychology. Watch me. I got a job as a substance abuse counselor. I began my master's degree and learned that the clinic where I worked supported a revolving door. I learned about co-occurring disorders. The whole person must be treated. I left not wanting to support knowing better without doing better. Arriving at Walter Reed, I was equipped with a master's degree. A neuropsychologist mentored me. I had another mentor, a marriage therapist, a sex therapist, and a pastor. I had another mentor who was a psychologist. I attended EMDR training. I added new skills. I sought certification and continued to grow, gain knowledge, and apply what I have learned.

If someone says you are born for something, that is great. But make sure that you continue to do the work that informs, confirms, and rehearses your greatness through your giftedness. From there, consider your brand recognition and your marketing messages. Develop that presentation that supports your credentials and testimonials that affirm your capabilities. Finally, activate your network to secure the customers, learning, or spiritual growth supporting your contribution.

Make sure to check out other titles By Arielle Nikol Jordan

Mindset Quality Workbook

www.ingramcontent.com/pod-product-compliance
Lightning Source LLC
Chambersburg PA
CBHW070133100426
42744CB00009B/1825